Fact Finders®

W9-BLR-450

HUMANS AND OUR PLANET

# HUMANS AND THE HYDROSPHERE

## Protecting Earth's Water Sources

by Ava Sawyer

DISCARD

CAPSTONE PRESS
a capstone imprint

MAY 2018

**Fact Finders Books are published by Capstone Press,**
**1710 Roe Crest Drive, North Mankato, Minnesota 56003**
**www.mycapstone.com**

Copyright © 2018 by Capstone Press, a Capstone imprint. All rights reserved. No part of this publication may be reproduced in whole or in part, or stored in a retrieval system, or transmitted in any form or by any means, electronic, mechanical, photocopying, recording, or otherwise, without written permission of the publisher.

**Library of Congress Cataloging-in-Publication Data**
Library of Congress Cataloging-in-Publication data is available on the Library of Congress website.

ISBN 978-1-5157-7198-2 (hardcover)
ISBN 978-1-5157-7212-5 (paperback)
ISBN 978-1-5157-7216-3 (eBook PDF)

The hydrosphere encompasses all water on Earth — from glaciers and ice to rivers and oceans. People use water everyday. How much water do you use? Find out how humans use water and

**Editorial Credits**
Editor: Nikki Potts
Designer: Philippa Jenkins
Media Researcher: Jo Miller
Production Specialist: Kathy McColley

**Photo Credits**
Alamy: Ronald Karpilo, 25; Shutterstock: Action Sports Photography, 21, Ammit Jack, 4, Angelo Giampiccolo, 12, Annzee, 11, AuntSpray, 15, B Brown, 18, corbac40, 24, Corepics VOF, 23 (top), CRSHELARE, 16, DoublePHOTO studio, 13, khwanchai, 7, Maciej Bledowski, 20, marekuliasz, 14, Matyas Rehak, 8, Michaelpuche, 10, Narin Nonthamand, 26–27, OPIS Zagreb, 5, Philip Pilosian, 17, Photodiem, cover, Rawpixel.com, throughout (background), Signature Message, 22-23, smereka, 9, Sue Burton PhotographyLtd, 19, wickerwood, 6

Printed and bound in China.
004655

# TABLE OF CONTENTS

R0451651921

MAY    2018

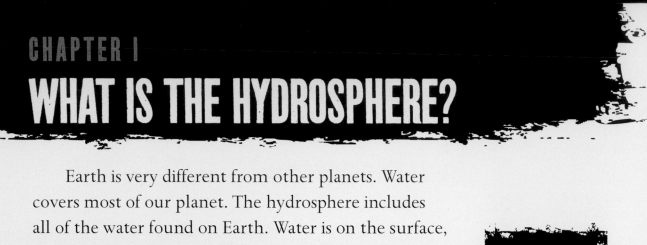

# CHAPTER 1
# WHAT IS THE HYDROSPHERE?

Earth is very different from other planets. Water covers most of our planet. The hydrosphere includes all of the water found on Earth. Water is on the surface, underground, in the air, and a part of every living thing. Water can be in the form of a liquid, solid, or gas. Life on Earth would not be possible without water.

Rivers, lakes, oceans, streams, and glaciers are all part of the hydrosphere.

Earth has five oceans: Pacific, Atlantic, Indian, Southern, and Arctic.

Earth's temperature allows most of the hydrosphere to be in liquid form. However, more than 97 percent of it is saltwater. Saltwater is unusable by most land animals, including humans. Oceans are large bodies of saltwater. They cover more than 70 percent of Earth and hold most of the planet's water. Oceans are the biggest part of the hydrosphere.

Freshwater is found either frozen, underground, or on Earth's surface in ponds, streams, rivers, and lakes.

## Oceans

The movement of the ocean is also a big part of the hydrosphere. Tides, currents, and waves move and mix the water. They help control Earth's climate while carrying life to every corner of the world. Tides affect the movement of the entire ocean. They are long waves that follow the moon's gravity. Tides cause shoreline sea levels to rise and fall twice every day.

The **water cycle** moves water within the hydrosphere. Water changes form throughout the cycle. The sun's energy **evaporates** surface water, mostly from the oceans. The water becomes vapor and forms clouds. It then condenses and falls back to Earth as rain or snow. Falling water — precipitation — shapes continents, fills lakes, and forms rivers. Water collects in these **reservoirs** and begins the cycle all over again. It is always moving, changing, and being reused all around our planet.

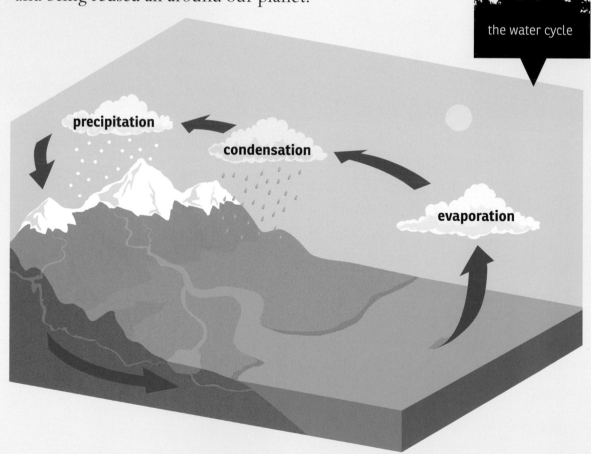

the water cycle

precipitation

condensation

evaporation

**water cycle**—how water changes as it travels around the world and moves between the ground and the air

**evaporate**—to change from a liquid into a vapor or gas

**reservoir**—a natural or artificial holding area for storing large amounts of water

As water moves through the water cycle, it changes phases. It can change between liquid, gas, and solid.

Earth's hydrosphere is a closed system. No water is added to or subtracted from it. The amount of water on Earth does not change over time. Today's water is the same water that existed during the time of the dinosaurs. Water is constantly in motion, being transformed and reused all over the planet. Water helps people, plants, and animals to survive. However, human activities are threatening the hydrosphere and the future of life on Earth.

## A Closed System

Because the water cycle circulates water from the surface of Earth to the atmosphere and back, the water supply seems to constantly renew itself. Still, garbage and pollution has made some freshwater undrinkable. Turning saltwater into drinking water is complicated and expensive. In addition, pollution threatens groundwater supplies. Groundwater is the main source of freshwater for much of the world's population. Contaminated groundwater can lead to a wide range of health problems. So even though the amount of water on Earth does not change, it is still important to conserve this resource.

# CHAPTER 2

# PEOPLE AND THE HYDROSPHERE

Water can be a source of entertainment. Many seek out sources of water for weekend activities. People travel to oceans, lakes, and rivers to relax and play. Public parks are often found near large bodies of water. People enjoy fishing, swimming, sailing, snorkeling, scuba diving, kayaking, canoeing, paddle boarding, and water skiing. Many enjoy ice skating in the winter. People also run, hike, bike, picnic, and camp around lakes. It is nice to enjoy water and the outdoors. It is also important to take care of them.

People of all ages snorkel on a coral reef in Sri Lanka.

Watering cattle is an indirect way people use water.

People are changing the hydrosphere. Many rely on water without understanding the hydrosphere and water cycle. Most people are not aware of the damage they cause to the hydrosphere. People are using up and destroying this valuable **natural resource**.

People use water every day for things such as drinking, bathing, cooking, and cleaning. These are direct uses of water. People also use water indirectly. Farmers use water for crops and livestock, which feed people. Companies and factories use water to make products they sell.

People also pollute water, often without understanding the consequences. **Contaminated** water harms life on Earth. Life cannot survive without clean water. Bodies of water are now shrinking, and usable water is becoming scarcer.

**natural resource**—a material found in nature that is useful to people
**contaminated**—unfit for use because of contact with a harmful substance

# CHAPTER 3

# HOW PEOPLE USE SURFACE WATER

Surface water is found aboveground. It makes up 0.25 percent of all the water on Earth. Oceans, lakes, and rivers are sources of surface water. People use 275 billion gallons (1 trillion liters) of surface water every day in the United States.

Bodies of water provide people with food. Fishers make their living on the water. Commercial fishing feeds families and communities all around the world. Healthier surface water means a healthier food supply.

Fishing is a common way of making a living along coastlines.

Hydroelectricity is a clean alternative energy source.

Surface water is also used to make power. People build dams to collect water. The trapped water is then channeled through power plants. The waves and currents of this water are moving energy. The moving water turns **turbines** that power generators that make electricity. **Hydroelectricity** powers many homes, towns, and cities.

**turbine**—a machine with blades that can be turned by wind, steam, or water
**hydroelectricity**—a form of energy caused by flowing water

People also build reservoirs to collect water. Reservoirs are huge human-made lakes that store water. First people use machinery to dig lake basins. Then they use dams to redirect river water. Reservoirs collect water during the rainy season and store it for the dry season. People use the reserves during times of drought. Larger populations have a greater need for reservoirs, especially in dry climates.

Surface water is important to industries worldwide. Most mining and manufacturing businesses use water during production. Factories and refineries often use energy from river water to power machines. Water cools machinery, and high-pressured water cleans it. Water is also used in the products being sold.

Marble-cutting factories use water to cool huge slabs of marble while being cut.

Barges often travel up and down rivers carrying heavy cargo.

Industrial companies use surface water to transport goods. People load boats, barges, and ferries with products and ship them all over the world. Traveling by water can be faster and cheaper than ground or air transportation.

# CHAPTER 4

# HOW PEOPLE USE GROUNDWATER

Groundwater is one of the largest sources of freshwater on Earth. It exists almost everywhere. Rain and melting snow seep into the ground. Groundwater slowly moves through layers of soil, sand, and rock. Trillions of gallons are stored in **aquifers** deep beneath the surface. The United States has an estimated 33,000 trillion gallons (125,000 trillion l) of groundwater. Some of this water has been underground for millions of years. But these groundwater reserves are shrinking.

## FACT

Ice makes up most of Earth's freshwater sources, but 96 percent of the remaining freshwater is groundwater.

A well supplies a water tank for cattle near Fort Collins, Colorado.

**aquifer**—an underground lake or stream of water

Americans use 80 billion gallons (303 billion l) of groundwater every day. Most people never think about groundwater because they cannot see it. Yet it is one of the most used natural resources on the planet. People dig wells in the ground and pump water to the surface. Most groundwater is used for agriculture, communities, and households.

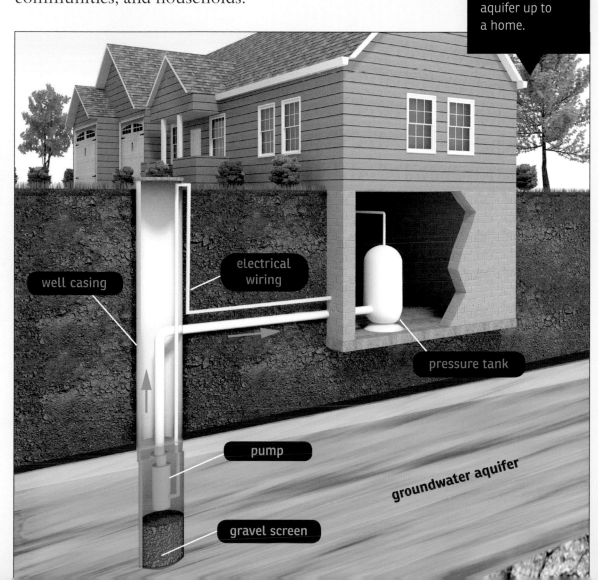

Water is pumped from an underground aquifer up to a home.

well casing

electrical wiring

pressure tank

pump

groundwater aquifer

gravel screen

Farmers use the most groundwater. People depend on farmers to grow food. Irrigating crops and raising livestock requires a lot of water. More than 60 percent of water used for irrigation comes from underground. In the United States, 54 billion gallons (204 billion l) of groundwater are used every day just on crops.

County and city water departments also use a lot of groundwater. They are the second-biggest water **consumers**. Communities store groundwater for public use. Water towers send water through underground pipes to homes, schools, and local businesses. Communities also use groundwater to fight fires, water lawns, fill pools, and clean roads.

Automatic irrigation systems are used to water fields.

**consumer**—a person who buys or uses products or services

Water towers hold large quantities of water that gets pumped out to homes and businesses.

Individual families are the third-largest consumers of groundwater. The average U.S. family uses 300 gallons (1,136 l) of groundwater every day. Most simply have to turn on a faucet. Half of the country depends on groundwater for drinking. In **rural** areas, groundwater supplies 99 percent of the drinking water. People also use groundwater to cook, clean, and shower.

## FACT

Washing machines and toilets use more water than any other appliance.

**rural**—having to do with the countryside or farming

# CHAPTER 5

# OVERCONSUMPTION

Water has many uses, but it is not distributed evenly around the world. That's why people collect it, store it, and move it. But having that control also makes it easier for people to take more water than they need. Overconsumption disrupts the balance of the entire hydrosphere.

Enough water is not always available for uses such as watering crops.

low water
levels at the
Upper Derwent
Reservoir in the
Peak District, UK

People are using more water than they should.
There is not enough freshwater to keep up with demand.
Nearly 70 percent of the world's freshwater is being used
just to grow food. By 2050 the demand for water is expected to rise
by 55 percent. That is twice as fast as population growth.

Most people are unknowingly wasteful with water. They leave
faucets and showers on too long. They use dishwashers and washing
machines when they are only half full.

Overconsumption is a serious problem. Many lakes, rivers, and
aquifers are getting smaller. They are being drained faster than the
water cycle can **replenish** them. It is affecting water supplies around
the world. People have thrown off the natural balance between the
hydrosphere and water cycle. Every little change affects the future of
water on Earth.

**replenish**—to make full again

# CHAPTER 6
# POLLUTION

Pollution harms the hydrosphere and the environment. Pollutants contaminate water and make it dangerous for plants, animals, and people.

Litter is the most obvious form of pollution. Litter is garbage people leave behind. It floats in water, covers shorelines, and gets stuck in sewer drains. Litter can come from people, and it can also come from landfills. Trash blows in the wind. It is carried across landscapes and eventually gets trapped in bodies of water.

While some litter, such as food, breaks down, plastics do not.

A crop duster sprays chemicals over a field.

Industrial waste is another form of pollution. Some companies dump harmful chemicals when they are done using them. The toxic waste seeps into groundwater and flows into oceans.

Farm chemicals also pollute groundwater and surface water. **Fertilizers** and **pesticides** flow with rainwater into streams, rivers, and lakes. Runoff pollutes water sources with unnatural nutrients. With the extra nutrients in the water, algae may grow out of control and kill fish.

## Pollution and Disease

Pollution is a serious problem around the world. Water sources are already extremely polluted in many countries. Polluted water breeds bacteria. It can cause outbreaks of deadly diseases. Waterborne diseases kill 14,000 people across the world every day! Nearly 1.5 billion people do not have access to clean drinking water.

**fertilizer**—a substance added to soil to make crops grow better

**pesticide**—a poisonous chemical used to kill insects, rats, and fungi that can damage plants

Oil spills are another form of pollution caused by people. People mine oil to use as an energy source. Huge oil reserves are found at the bottom of the ocean. Oil companies build large drilling rigs in the ocean to extract the oil. Pipes sometimes break and spill oil into the water. Oil floats on the surface and spreads quickly. It is hard to contain and even harder to clean up. The greasy pollutant sticks to everything. Oil contaminates water, kills marine animals, and destroys shorelines.

Crews work to clean up an oil spill in Ao Prao Beach at Samet Island.

Oil spills affect animals such as birds, fish, and other ocean wildlife.

# GLOBAL WARMING

People turn mined oil into gas. Gas is burned to fuel cars, and cars pollute the air with exhaust smoke. Smoke is filled with the harmful greenhouse gas, carbon dioxide. Greenhouse gases trap heat in the atmosphere. They are responsible for **global warming**.

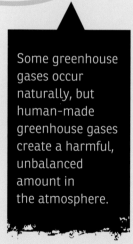

Global warming has a huge impact on water. Trapped heat warms the planet. Higher temperatures speed up the water cycle, and water evaporates faster. Clouds have less time to travel before heavy rains fall. Water is falling back to Earth in the same place where it evaporated. This changes the distribution of water in the hydrosphere. Wet climates are flooding, and dry climates are experiencing droughts and wildfires.

Global warming is melting Earth's glacial ice. Ice is the second-largest water source in the hydrosphere. It is frozen freshwater. It would turn salty if it melted into the ocean.

Some greenhouse gases occur naturally, but human-made greenhouse gases create a harmful, unbalanced amount in the atmosphere.

**global warming**—the idea that Earth's temperature is slowly rising

Sea levels would rise by 230 feet (70 meters) if all the ice melted. Islands and coastlines would be underwater. Hundreds of millions of people would be homeless and forced to move inland. There would be less land to grow crops and raise livestock.

The Muir Glacier in Alaska slowly melted between 1899 to 2003.

## Ice Sheet

Ice sheets alone hold 99 percent of the freshwater on the planet. They form in polar regions that are flat and high in elevation. The two polar ice sheets on Earth today cover Greenland and Antarctica. They store enormous amounts of water. Ice sheets grow when more snow falls than melts. The weight slowly changes the snow from powder to hard ice crystals. Layers of ice compact and get denser over thousands of years. They eventually turn into solid ice. Ice sheets move like liquid water — although much more slowly — and greatly impact the landscape. They shift and slide over everything in their paths. Ice sheets cover entire mountains, valleys, and plains.

# CHAPTER 7
# HOW CAN HUMANS HELP?

The hydrosphere sustains all life on Earth. What people put in the water and how they use it affects the future of the entire planet. Many people may not realize how important water is until it's gone. Water is required for life. People, plants, and animals cannot survive without it.

A crew works to clean up litter from a beach in Thailand.

Populations around the world need to work together to save Earth's water. The only **sustainable** solution is to use less water and clean up pollution. Here are a few ways you can help. Turn off faucets and take shorter showers. Encourage your family, friends, and neighbors to save water too. Recycle bottles, cans, metals, papers, and cardboard. Making these small changes will lessen the amount of trash in landfills and in the water. Buying organic food and natural products will also help the hydrosphere. It will reduce chemical runoff that flows into drinking water. The choices you make every day affect the future of the hydrosphere.

**sustainable**—done in a way that can be continued and that doesn't use up natural resources

# TIMELINE

**1970**

December 2nd, the Environmental Protection Agency (EPA) is established.

**1976**

Congress passes the Toxic Substances Control Act (TSCA). It provides the EPA the authority to protect public health and the environment through controls on toxic chemicals.

**1980**

Water in Duluth, Minnesota, is so polluted that people are forced to use only bottled water.

**1987**

The Water Quality Act requires the EPA to regulate storm water runoff and requires states to prepare approved plans to control non-point source pollution.

**1989**

Exxon Valdez spills 11 million gallons (42 million l) of crude oil into Alaska's Prince William Sound.

**1990**

Congress passes the Pollution Prevention Act. The act focuses on source reduction.

**1990**

Congress passes the Oil Pollution Act to better prepare and be able to respond to potential oil spills.

**1994**

The Safe Drinking Water Act establishes drinking water standards.

**2010**

An explosion causes the Deepwater Horizon oil rig to sink. Oil gushes into the Gulf of Mexico for 87 days. Over 130 million gallons (490 million l) of oil is spilled.

**2014**

Flint, Michigan, changes its water source to the Flint River from the Detroit River, spurring a water crisis in the city.

# GLOSSARY

**aquifer** (AK-wuh-fuhr)—an underground lake or stream of water

**consumer** (kuhn-SOO-muhr)—a person who buys or uses products or services

**contaminated** (kuhn-TA-muh-nay-tuhd)—unfit for use because of contact with a harmful substance

**evaporate** (i-VA-puh-rayt)—to change from a liquid into a vapor or gas

**fertilizer** (FUHR-tuh-ly-zuhr)—a substance added to soil to make crops grow better

**global warming** (GLOHB-uhl WORM-ing)—the idea that Earth's temperature is slowly rising

**hydroelectricity** (hye-droh-i-lek-TRISS-uh-tee)—a form of energy caused by flowing water

**natural resource** (NACH-ur-uhl REE sorss)—a material found in nature that is useful to people

**pesticide** (PES-tuh-side)—a poisonous chemical used to kill insects, rats, and fungi that can damage plants

**replenish** (ri-PLEN-ish)—to make full again

**reservoir** (REZ-uh-vwar)—a natural or artificial holding area for storing large amounts of water

**rural** (RUR-uhl)—having to do with the countryside or farming

**sustainable** (suh-STAY-nuh-buhl)—done in a way that can be continued and that doesn't use up natural resources

**turbine** (TUR-bine)—a machine with blades that can be turned by wind, steam, or water

**water cycle** (WAH-tur SY-kuhl)—how water changes as it travels around the world and moves between the ground and the air

# READ MORE

Enz, Tammy. *Liquid Planet: Exploring Water on Earth with Science Projects*. Discover Earth Science. North Mankato, Minn.: Capstone Press, 2016.

Feinstein, Stephen. *Drying Up: Running Out of Water*. The End of Life as We Know It. New York: Enslow Publishing, 2016.

Iyer, Rani. *Endangered Rivers: Investigating Rivers in Crisis*. Endangered. North Mankato, Minn.: Capstone Press, 2015.

# INTERNET SITES

FactHound offers a safe, fun way to find Internet sites related to this book. All of the sites on FactHound have been researched by our staff.

Here's all you do:

Visit *www.facthound.com*

Type in this code: 9781515771982

Super-cool stuff! Check out projects, games and lots more at **www.capstonekids.com**

# CRITICAL THINKING QUESTIONS

- Explain how the water moves through the water cycle.

- People pollute water sources through the use of fertilizers and pesticides. What are fertilizers and pesticides?

- What are some effects of global warming?

# INDEX